12 Elements of Account Management Success:

A Practical Guide on How to Add Value to Your Company with Structured Account Management

12 Elements of Account Management Success:

A Practical Guide on How to Add Value to Your Company with Structured Account Management

Ezra Schneier

2019

Copyright © 2019 by Ezra Schneier

All rights reserved. This book or any portion thereof may not be reproduced or used in any manner whatsoever without the express written permission of the publisher except for the use of brief quotations in a book review or scholarly journal.

First Printing: 2019

ISBN 978-1-79473-621-4

Dedication

To Account Managers.

At the end of the day, you make businesses successful.

And at the end of the day, there is often a feeling of success.

Contents

Preface xi

Introduction 15

Chapter 1: Make it a Package 19

Chapter 2: Welcome Aboard Communication 22

Chapter 3. Strategy Statement 25

Chapter 4: Account Management Guide 29

Chapter 5: Client Charter 33

Chapter 6: Client-Specific Account Plan 36

Chapter 7: Early-Action Review 46

Chapter 8: After-Action Review (AAR) 48

Chapter 9: Quarterly and Annual Reviews 53

Chapter 10: Client Satisfaction Survey 61

Chapter 11: Renewal and Expansion Plan 68

Chapter 12: Executive Sponsorship 70

Chapter 13: The Scorecard 74

Chapter 14: Internal Communication 77

Chapter 15: Summary 78

Appendix 1 – Sample Job Descriptions 79

12 Elements of Account Management Success
1. Welcome Aboard Communication
2. Strategy Statement
3. Account Management Guide - Overall Account Management Plan
4. Client Charter
5. Client-Specific Account Plan
6. Early Action Review
7. After-Action Review (AAR)
8. Quarterly Business Reviews (QBR) and Annual Reviews
9. Client Satisfaction Survey
10. Renewal and Expansion Plan
11. Executive Sponsorship
12. The Scorecard

Preface

Account Management is a critical business function. But it is frequently overlooked.

Account Management is usually not given enough credit for the success of a business.

Often, account management is thought of as something that can just get done without a clear strategy and plan. At many organizations conventional wisdom has it that account management does not require serious investment and recognition. Managers who feel this way are badly mistaken.

A major reason for chariness with account management is that many companies have not solidified the function. They have not stated and demonstrated the virtues of account management in a way that is understood by all stakeholders, including executive leadership.

Smart companies and leaders know that account management is a pillar of success. In fact, they make it part of their identity and brand promise.

While consumers and employees at companies buy products and services because of particular characteristics, they often remain customers because of their client experience. This is directly related to Account Management. A positive client experience is the result of a thoughtful, structured plan designed to deliver value and create customer loyalty.

The main purpose of this book is to help you develop a sharply defined account management function. Or to help you revise and enhance the elements of what you have in place. That is, go from your current state to an end state that includes a more structured, consistent account management process that is clearly recognized within your company and by your customers.

There is a spectrum of specific items an organization can implement to make account management a solid aspect of the business. In this short book we have chosen twelve specific items to review with the hope that there is something for everyone in that array.

Account Management is hard work which is sometimes unappreciated. When account management is done right, it can be highly rewarding for all stakeholders: Company, Client and the Account Manager. While the emphasis here is on business to business account management, the concepts can apply in other types of companies, too.

In their classic book, *The New Successful Large Account Management: Maintaining and Growing Your Most Important Assets – Your Customers*, authors Robert Miller and Stephen Heiman, put it this way:

> Whatever their size and whatever their markets, businesses everywhere need to protect their key account "assets." They need to deliver real customer value or risk being "de-positioned" as commodity suppliers. They need to invest appropriately in the strategic relationships that are the only safeguard against account erosion.[1]

On a personal note, I have been inspired by many in the Account Management Profession. Their creativity, enthusiasm and passion for success are extraordinary traits that deserve more appreciation.

---

[1] Robert B. Miller, Stephen E. Heiman, Tad Tuleja, *The New Successful Large Account Management: Maintaining and Growing Your Most Important Assets – Your Customers*, (New York, NY: Grand Central Publishing, April 2005), p. xvii.

Since you are reading this book, you are probably already in the account management field or interested in exploring new ways to improve account management at your company. Maybe you feel there is potential for improvement or want to accelerate your progress in this area.

I hope you find useful information here that can be applied to your situation.

At its core, the goal of this book is to offer a framework for account management. Recognizing the premise that success in account management means having a thoughtful, organized plan that is fully embraced by customers and internal stakeholders, in these pages we seek to offer suggestions that can be used in your role. Simply put, our goal is to impart specific ways that your account management program can be developed or improved.

A key point that will be noted in these pages is the necessity to have a structured, repeatable process in place for successful account management. By choosing practical elements to include in your account management process - and making sure they are consistently applied - the full program will be sustainable.

> ✓ Consistently carry out the account management process.
> ✓ Work to let everyone know about the elements of the process you use.

A successful program includes customers, internal managers and staff, partners – everyone. By building this awareness, your process becomes a standard and expected way of doing business. This is the result you want. Having a consistent, structured approach will allow you to achieve success.

In our experience, almost all customers give significant value to account management. Having a clear framework – the standard – and making it part of a company's culture is what we are focused on here.

After reading this book, it is the author's hope that you will put in place a structured account management program. It does not have to have everything you want to ultimately include. Some elements can be added over time. But it should have the core pieces that can be carried out at your company at this point in time.

Even if one or two of the ideas suggested here are adopted by your organization, we will consider it a win.

Introduction

Account Management is a key ingredient for the success of any business. How we treat clients and how we collaborate with clients can make a huge difference in the value that is created for our employers.

In these pages we will focus on specific ways to build collaboration and lasting, trusting relationships with clients. At the same time, we will try to demonstrate the importance of having a clear plan with defined expectations that are fully understood within your organization and by the customer. Consider this a framework that can be used in the design or refinement of your account management process.

This book sets out to highlight twelve specific ways to achieve success with account management. In writing this book, it is the goal to share proven ways that account management can add value to your organization. At the same time, we set out to help the account manager shine.

Of course, all twelve elements described here may not apply to every company. That's fine. Pick what you feel can bring you the most value and what works for you.

It is the main premise of this book that the value of Account Management can be enhanced by bringing an organized approach to the function. It is easy to take a more casual style and react to the day-to-day events that take place. Put out today's fires. That is usually the wrong path to follow. Having a well thought out plan and consistently following that plan leads to stronger client relationships.

Executing the plan with all of its components has the advantage of showing clients you are committed to their success. You have developed a recipe that works and you are putting it into action. Done right, this will become part of your company's identity. New customers will be won. Existing customers will be more loyal because of your approach.

When we talk about executing the plan, it is worth referring to the work of Larry Bossidy (former Chairman and CEO of Honeywell) and Ram Charan (author and adviser). Bossidy and Charan wrote the book *Execution: The Discipline of Getting Things Done*, which became a NY Times Bestseller. They define execution this way:

> Execution is a Discipline. People think of execution as the tactical side of business. That's the first big mistake. Tactics are central to execution, but execution is not tactics. Execution is fundamental to strategy and has to shape it. No worthwhile strategy can be planned without taking into account the organization's ability to execute it. If you're talking about the smaller specifics of getting things done, call the process implementation, or sweating the details, or whatever you want to. But don't confuse execution with tactics.[2]

Bossidy and Charan suggest that the lack of execution is the main reason companies fall short of their promises. We think of structured account management as a discipline. With proper execution it leads to success and serves as a strong differentiator for the organization.

Account Management is not a fad. Successful companies make structured account management a foundation of doing business. Supplying a terrific customer experience can make a positive difference in the long term. It can be the source of growth, increased revenue and profitability. That is not going to change.

---

[2] Larry Bossidy, Ram Charan, *Execution: The Discipline of Getting Things Done*, (New York, NY: Crown Business, 2002), pp. 21-22.

Therefore, it is worth paying attention to getting account management right. In the popular business advice book *Rework*, authors Jason Fried and David Heinemeier Hansson give short, practical suggestions on how to succeed at business. The authors are the founders of the software company, 37signals. For example, they tell readers to "focus on what won't change." Get the basics right and that will make you strong.

Focus on what won't change

A lot of companies focus on the next big thing. They latch on to what's hot and new. They follow the latest trends and technology.

That's a fool's path. You start focusing on fashion instead of substance. You start paying attention to things that are constantly changing instead of things that last.

The core of your business should be built around things that won't change. Things that people are going to want today *and* ten years from now. Those are the things you should invest in.

Amazon invests in fast, free shipping, great selection, friendly return policies, and affordable prices. These things will always be in high demand.

Japanese automakers also focus on core principles that don't change: reliability, affordability, and practicality. People wanted those things thirty years ago, they want them today, and they'll want them thirty years from now.

For 37signals, things like speed, simplicity, ease of use, and clarity are our focus. Those are timeless desires. People aren't going to wake up in ten years and say,

'Man, I wish software was harder to use.' They won't say, 'I wish this application was slower.'

Remember, fashion fades away. When you focus on *permanent* features, you're in bed with things that never go out of style.[3]

It is worth noting the research shows that focus may not be enough. In his book *Great at Work*, Morten Hansen points out that success is amplified by choosing a few priorities (focus) and then obsessing over those items. That is, apply significant effort to those specific chosen areas.

The obsessing part is key to getting the desired results.

We believe companies that obsess over account management will be the ones that stand out in the market. They will deliver the greatest value to customers - and achieve success for their own organizations.

---

[3] Jason Fried and David Heinemeier Hansson, *Rework*, (New York, NY: Crown Business, 2010), p.85.

Chapter 1: Make it a Package

If there is just one point we hope readers take away from these pages it is to make your account management activities into a package. I believe that is a key to success for account managers. It shifts account management from defense to offense. The package puts down an established set of things that will be done. Customers know it. Stakeholders know it. You know it.

To do this:
   a. Identify the key elements of what you do in your account management function.
   b. Write them in a list with a one sentence description of each.
   c. Give this document a name – For example: *Account Management Guide, Account Management Description, Working Together, Client Success, Our Relationship Handbook.*
   d. Share this document with your internal colleagues and customers.

This package will change over time. You can add to it and make adjustments. Maybe you even have two or three packages to choose from. This can be based on size of customer - or other criteria. But have a package of Account Management elements to use as soon as practical.

Start with what you do now. Turn your set of account management activities into a package offering.

Why is this a big deal?

Simply put, account management is frequently unstructured. Putting it into a package makes it more organized, tangible and adds clarity - for customers and internal stakeholders.

It is also worth considering that *not* having a package of elements to use in your account management program can be seen as unprofessional. This can arouse suspicion about the proficiency and ability of the Account Manager. With this in mind, we hope you are convinced that there are multiple reasons to implement a package approach to your account management program.

Central to the package of elements is the value delivered:

- ✓ To the customer: In this package are the things you can expect to receive with consistency to support our relationship.

- ✓ To the internal manager and your colleagues: In this package are the items we are committed to doing – with regularity and for good purpose.

When working with a vendor, partner or supplier, organizations are often not fully aware of what they should expect to receive from their account manager (or another title for person responsible for the relationship at the company.)

The package takes away the mystery and makes it clear.

Internally, your team may not understand what you do. And they may not get the process that is followed to bring positive account management results. Having a package of elements allows you to be proactive and bring shape to what you are doing.

The package explains what is going on.

As you read this book, there may be items described here that can be added to your playbook and included in the package.

Customers will appreciate knowing what is in the package. So will managers. And having the package will keep everyone on the same page.

Done right, this can be a powerful differentiator for your company. Believe it or not, a large number of companies do not offer a package. Based on experience, having a package is an ingredient for success.

Here is a checklist of the 12 Elements of Account Management Success that will be described in this brief handbook:

1. Welcome Aboard Communication
2. Strategy Statement
3. Account Management Guide - Overall Account Management Plan
4. Client Charter
5. Client-Specific Account Plan
6. Early Action Review
7. After-Action Review (AAR)
8. Quarterly Business Reviews (QBR) and Annual Reviews
9. Client Satisfaction Survey
10. Renewal and Expansion Plan
11. Executive Sponsorship
12. The Scorecard

As noted earlier, the package does not have to include all of these twelve elements. Pick the ones that make the most sense for you at this point in time and make it your offering – *your own package*.

Chapter 2: Welcome Aboard Communication

When you have a new client, the Account Manager has an opportunity to set the table with clear expectations about what the customer can expect in terms of their account management journey and experience. There should be a communication – likely an e-mail – that outlines the package. This is the Welcome Aboard Communication from the Account Manager.

Some organizations like to have this communication be supportive of a customer's transition from sales to account management. This helps establish a clear understanding of the key points of contact going forward.

The Welcome Aboard Communication describes – in a quick outline - what the client will receive in the coming weeks and months. At this point, it is best to keep the communication short and focused on the account management approach that is to be followed. Try to steer clear of making it bulky and too detailed. That will dilute the message.

Timing is important. Ideally, have the communication delivered the day the client signs the contract with your company.

Maybe you already do this. If so, great. The top reason people tell us they do not do this is they say it is covered in other ways by their organization. For example:

- *We address all of that in the kickoff meeting - there is a slide that covers it...*
- *Sales already told the customer all of this...*
- *Other things are more important to communicate*
- *There is no need for a separate e-mail about this.... they get too many e-mails as it is...*

- *It may cause confusion or inconsistency in our messaging...*

In my view, these are not valid. A clear communication from the Account Manager on the specific topic of account management expectations is valued by your clients and supports the work you plan to do going forward.

If you are faced with this type of objection, try to make the point that you feel the communication is truly important and sets the course for the overall relationship to follow. Explain to your colleagues:

- ✓ Value proposition of having a structured account management program;
- ✓ Laying out the design of that plan early in the relationship supports the overall program and gets everyone off to a positive start
- ✓ Shows commitment to serious account management
- ✓ Builds respect for the account management function by customers.

See a sample welcome aboard communication on the next page.

From: Edward Cleveland

To: Kathy Ellenmore

Re: **Welcome Aboard as a New Client of GreatCo: Account Management Outline**

Kathy,

This is a quick note to thank you for choosing GreatCo to meet your marketing technology goals. We are delighted to have the opportunity to work with you and your fine team.

All of us at GreatCo look forward to supplying outstanding service and exceeding your expectations.

Besides terrific technology, we are totally committed to providing a high level of personal attention to you as a valued client. Through constant improvements and innovation, we look forward to delivering the services and innovation you need - now and in the future.

Account Management

Clients value our organized approach to account management. As your Client Success Manager, I am committed to delivering the elements that can bring you the best results. These are the standard items I suggest we start with:

- Client Charter

- Account Plan

- Quarterly Business Reviews

Please suggest a date and time that fits your schedule in the next week so we can have an introductory call and I can gather the necessary information to prepare the draft Client Charter for your review.

Thank you.

Chapter 3. Strategy Statement

A critical step for Account Managers is creating an ***Account Management Strategy Statement***. This does not have to be elaborate. In fact, it can be very brief, just one page. But it must be written down and shared with all stakeholders at your company. This has the benefit of everyone involved seeing and committing to the model.

Basically, the Account Management Strategy answers the question: *Why?* Let's take just a moment to look at the big picture. A clear, structured account management approach will contribute to strong business results. It can have two main components:

a. Employees. The strategy sets the tone for how the company views its role and cares for team members. Why it exists, what it believes in. We know that associates who enjoy their jobs are more productive and creative. They wake up and go home happier and more engaged. They treat their co-workers and customers well - and they drive long-lasting success.

b. Customers. Customers want to do business with organizations with great products and services - and people they trust. This produces customer loyalty, inspires customers to tell others about their positive experiences. In turn, this creates growth and the attainment of goals.

So, the Account Management Strategy will address the company's two key constituents: Employees and Customers. It will quickly explain that the approach to account management has a clear purpose. It will clearly answer: *Why?*

Besides getting buy-in from a company's leaders and others, the Strategy Statement is an opportunity to frame the purpose of account management in a way that demonstrates its importance.

This is a chance to clearly state why account management really matters. The statement should say how the company benefits from structured account management.

Michael Porter, the well-known author and Harvard Business School professor, has written extensively about competitive strategies and creating a competitive advantage. Differentiation is a type of competitive advantage. Companies differentiate themselves from competitors by supplying something unique that is of value to buyers. The proper type of differentiation always creates value for customers. Structured account management is a way to deliver real value and standout from the field of competitors.

In his book, *Competitive Advantage: Creating and Sustaining Superior Performance*, Porter writes:

> Differentiation cannot be understood by viewing the firm in aggregate, but stems from the specific activities a firm performs and how they affect the buyer. Differentiation grows out of the firm's value chain. Virtually any value activity is a potential source of uniqueness. The procurement of raw materials and other inputs can affect the performance of the end product and hence differentiation. For example, Heineken pays particular attention to the quality and purity of the ingredients for its beer and uses a constant strain of yeast. Similarly, Steinway uses skilled technicians to choose the finest materials for its pianos, and Michelin is more selective than its competitors about the grades of rubber it uses in its tires.[4]

---

[4] Michael E. Porter, *Competitive Advantage: Creating and Sustaining Superior*

Following Porter's advice, we can use the Strategy Statement to show how account management is a differentiator that creates value for customers, makes our company special and contributes directly to success. This level of importance is more than account management often gets at many companies. Two suggestions when writing your Strategy Statement:

- Give weight to the function as an important business function for your company.
- Frame account management as a unique differentiator with high value for customers.

At its core, the Strategy Statement describes the overall goals that are expected with Account Management and can list the basic elements used in your account management program.

It may be shared with clients, too. In fact, it can be extremely beneficial to share the strategy statement with clients - and even prospective clients. This openness lets everyone know:

- There is a strong belief in quality account management;
- A cohesive program is in place;
- What to expect as a client;
- Expressing a commitment to continuous improvement and understanding of priorities.

The important thing is to have clarity about what it is you want to achieve with account management and the key elements of the program. Following is an example.

Performance, (New York: The Free Press, 1985), pp. 120-121.

Account Management Strategy Statement

ABC Company is committed to helping clients succeed in their business.

One way we do this is through structured and proactive Account Management.

This includes:

- Developing a clear understanding of the requirements and goals of our clients.

- Regular communication about the services and products being delivered.

- Routine reviews of the relationship between our companies.

- Understanding of priorities.

- Using measurements to track progress.

We believe in developing lasting relationships with clients built on trust and delivering value. To do this, we have developed an organized approach to Account Management which serves as a critical part of our business relationship with clients.

Our team members are highly valued. Account Management associates are critical to our success and growth.

Chapter 4: Account Management Guide

Once the strategy is set, an **Account Management Guide** should be developed. This is the overall business plan for your account management function. It will list the activities that are to be done in carrying out the Account Management function along with a short description of each element.

Having a clear Account Management Guide – a playbook – is a best practice to include in your portfolio. Essentially, it is the list of elements that make up your package. You may want to add some narrative to explain what you seek to accomplish in carrying out the elements. But it is a guide to what you will do, what customers will receive. And it is useful for other stakeholders to gain a full understanding of the content you have determined will help achieve your objectives.

Establishing an Account Management Guide with a set of meaningful activities will help enable you to stay relevant to customers. And it can help your organization be seen as a proactive, market-leader that deploys a structured and serious approach.

The guide can be a checklist or a more detailed document with a full explanation of the practices to be accomplished. Having this guide defines what is to be done in relation to Account Management. This should also be shared and agreed to internally by the appropriate people. In addition, the Account Management Guide provides the framework for what clients will experience. It serves as a review of what they can expect from doing business with your company.

Some companies divide their clients into groups or tiers. For example, the top 10 or 20 clients may be the Tier 1 – or Strategic

Accounts - and the rest of the clients considered normal accounts. The idea of the segmentation is to clearly identify those clients which are the most valuable to your business. Of course, this takes into consideration the current revenue attributable to each client. Also, the potential for future growth can be a factor. For instance, you may work with one division of a client and have an opportunity to expand that relationship. This situation may warrant labeling that company as a strategic account.

Besides being a top revenue contributor, or the potential to be in those ranks, there may be other reasons to classify a client as a strategic account. For example, there may have been a product or service issue that occurred and giving the client status as a Strategic Account may be a way to mitigate the risk of losing the relationship.

The following is a sample Account Management Guide. Remember the elements to include are determined based on your situation.

Sample Account Management Guide

This guide is a summary of the activities we are committed to doing in support of our Account Management strategy.

Client Charter Strategy Statement Value Vision	Every Account Manager should have a strategic Value Vision for where and how you can help customers achieve their business goals. A recap of the strategic business goals each specific customer seeks to achieve from using our services. While the account team needs to create the initial draft, it also should be reviewed and modified in collaboration with the customer to best reflect the impact they value most. The Account Value Vision helps ensure that the account team is aligned with the strategy of their customers.
Client-Specific Account Plan	A summary of the priorities of each client in using our services. And how we will accomplish them.
Quarterly Business Reviews (QBR)	Account Managers should conduct a Quarterly Business Review with key people. In this meeting, you can highlight insights learned from operations and experiences doing business together. Also, discuss the most important initiatives underway at the client to determine if there is a way to help contribute to success. This is designed to directly support the overall relationship.

Client Satisfaction Surveys	An annual (or semi-annual) brief survey to learn how customers view our service and to see trends.
The Scorecard	A set of KPIs with customers that are measured and jointly reviewed every six months. This includes operational metrics, as well as business metrics, enabling us to measure and leverage both operational performance and financial impact.

Chapter 5: Client Charter

It is recommended that each client have a **Client Charter**. This is a one-page recap of their business goals and how using your product or service is aligned with those goals. The Client Charter is always presented to the client for their review and input. It is a best practice to ask the client to make sure you got it right and to mark-up the Charter.

The Charter can be presented to brand new clients or existing customers. We have found that this allows the company to make sure that you understand why the client bought from you and their business priorities. It is meant to be a high-level review of the customer's goals and expectations.

Because it covers only the fundamentals without a great amount of detail, a Client Charter is fairly fast and easy to produce for each customer. We have seen this element of the Account Management Plan produce outsize returns and strongly recommend it be given serious consideration.

Over time, say annually, the Account Manager should review the Client Charter with the client and update the document.

Clients appreciate the Charter. It sends a strong message that you understand their goals and what they want from your company and its team.

Following is an example Client Charter.

February 20, 2020

To: Patricia Tobaff, Manager of Operations

Fm: Stephen Valli

Re: SPP, Inc. – Client Success Charter (Draft)

Patricia,

Following our discussion, below is the SPP Client Success Charter for your review. We would value your thoughts and suggestions. Please consider this a draft.

1. Purpose

As part of the Harbor Company approach to Client Success we supply clients with a brief **Charter**. The idea is to summarize our understanding of your goals with regard to supply chain technology solutions – and your logistics more broadly. This helps make sure we are fully aligned with your key objectives.

Also included are a few specific items related to our technology solutions. It is our goal in having this Charter to make sure Harbor is aware of, and aligned with, the strategic objectives and desires of SPP.

2. **SPP Goals - 2020**

a. Introduce more automation and efficiency. SPP desires to have more automation in its supply chain management practices and processes to gain efficiencies. Reduce off-line processes through greater automation and technology. Replace spreadsheets and manual off-line work with automation.
b. Make it easier for managers to determine, review and plan for supply chain decisions in connection with logistics, transportation operations and international cargo movement.
c. Have an automated workflow and approval process for supply chain planning and decision-making.
d. Introduce automated transportation documents and statements for internal needs, customers and government compliance requirements.
e. Use management reporting derived from information in the system to review transportation movements and other items associated with aggregated data.

3. **Solutions**

a. Harbor Connection v32 will be configured and implemented.
b. Manager training and User Guides will be developed.
c. Success measurements will be put in place to track results.

Chapter 6: Client-Specific Account Plan

The Client Charter, described in the previous chapter, is a high-level review of the main goals your client wants to achieve as a result of the relationship. Think of it as a summary of the strategic goals - or the business goals - an organization desires to accomplish by working with you.

The **Client-Specific Account Plan** on the other hand covers the nitty gritty. It is a review of what is to be done in the near and mid-term for a customer.

Why Are Account Plans Frequently Missing?

Too often, there is not an individualized Client Account Plan for every customer. In many ways, this is the most important item for the customer and the Account Manager. We think it is essential for every customer - or at least for every significant customer.

If it is so important, why is it missing in so many cases? We see three common reasons. The first reason the Client Account Plan does not exist is that some companies treat them as internal-only plans. That is, they never share them with customers. When that is the case, there is no obligation to present the plan to customers. And they are skipped. To overcome this impediment, organizations should tell customers up-front, even when they are prospects, that they will receive an Account Plan in the ordinary course of doing business.

Second reason: Customer Tiers. If customer tiers do not exist, and there is a mix of large and small customers, the creation of Account Plans becomes viewed as a ponderous task. The solution: focus on the large customers, Tier 1, and commit to producing

Account Plans for that segment of your customer base. The lower tiers can have a standard, off-the shelf plan.

The third reason why Account Plans sometimes do not exist in an organization is that Account Managers try to overthink what the plan should contain. And this leads to not completing the plan. The solution: Make it simple. It does not have to be long and elaborate. If you make it simple it is easier to complete, present to stakeholders, put in place and execute. And it will get done.

Occam's razor holds that the simplest explanation is often the correct one. That principle often applies to account management.

A Client-Specific Account Plan should be able to be developed in about an hour. An Account Manager with 40 clients would be investing 40 hours of effort to have them all completed. At a pace of one per day, all Account Plans are written in 40 days – two months. Once they are developed the next step is sharing them with your internal team, and the relevant clients.

The Plan: Keep It Short and Simple

We like to think of the Account Plan as having three parts:

a. A short list of the top things that must be done to keep the client's business. These are the specific things that are profoundly important to you and your customer. Emphasis on customer. There are items you would like to do to further your business relationship, too. But start with what is most important to the customer.

b. A description of what you are specifically going to do for the customer.

c. An explanation of how those items will be accomplished.

If we think about the Account Plan in these three basic sections, we can easily review the identified areas and share with stakeholders our collective priorities. In addition, we can easily monitor if these continue to be the right focus items over time and measure how we are tracking for success and making a difference for the client.

With this in mind we come up with basic account plan examples shown on the following pages.

Basic Account Plan: Telling Corporation

Top Client Priorities	Addressing the Priority	How the Items will be Accomplished	Measuring Success
Have an on-line solution for customers to submit suggestions to the company. Allow other customers to vote on the suggestions. Let all customers see and track the development of selected suggestions and learn about their introduction.	Implement cloud-based My Idea Tracker Software, Version 3.9.	Requirements gathering and analysis. Project plan for configuration. Implementation and activation	
Roll out and communicate with customers about the availability of the product by September 2020.	Work with the designated Engagement Manager for execution of the Activation and Launch Plan.	Activation and Launch Plan for internal stakeholders and customers: • Training • Design content on site • Examples	

Strategic Account Plan

Name of Client

Business Overview

Annual Account Targets

Client's Key Priorities

Client's Key Initiatives

Client's Key People

Product and Revenue

Action Plan

Product	Est. Annual Revenue	Our Value Proposition	Actions	Owner	Timeline

Prepared By: _____ Date: ___ / ___ / ___

An Expanded Account Plan

While we have just looked at a basic Account Plan that can be adapted for your clients and your organization, there are definitely situations where you want to expand the plan.

That is great. But please avoid delaying the implementation of a plan while the perfectly crafted one is being designed.

If this is new for you and your organization, pay the most attention to getting something going that you can use and hits on the key items that are important to you and your company – the priorities.

With the expanded version, you may want to include more information about the client, their business and strategy. Also, how you can expand the relationship by introducing new products or extending the use of certain ones in more divisions or business units.

The following is an example of a more detailed Account Plan that contains additional information and sections than in our basic model.

Sample
Expanded Client-Specific Account Plan

A) Where are we?

Discuss where you and your customer are in your relationship.

- What is going well?
- What is a challenge?
- What needs improvement?
- What are the key measurements of success?
- How does performance compare to benchmarks?
- Are things getting better or getting worse?

B) Where do we want to go?

Where can we get the most value going forward?   Near-Term, Mid-Term and Long-Term. What are the priorities in each category?

- What is the overall purpose or objective?
- What is the main goal desired from the relationship?
- At this point, assess the relationship.
- What are the top one or two things we desire to change to enhance the relationship?
- What is the biggest issue being faced by the client in connection with your product or service?
- What can we do about it?
- What new solutions can be introduced?

C) What changes have to be made?

What does success look like? How can we achieve success together? What's standing in the way?

- What would it take to improve how it is going now?
- What are the risks (internal/external)?
- What is in or out of your control
- What would create more opportunities?
- What do you need to stop or start doing?
- How can you improve performance?
- Consider alternatives. Options A, B and C?
- What are the quick wins? Sometimes a small change can have a big impact.

D) Who is involved? Stakeholders

Who are the people to become involved in the relationship? What do they need to do? How are you going to get their support?

- Consider the who, what, when and how needed to make your strategy a reality.
- Should your focus be narrow or wide?
- Can your primary contacts coordinate meetings with others in the organization?
- Is there a value proposition or initiative that will help make those meetings happen?

E) Budget

What is the budget for this year and the next three years?

F) How should progress be measured?

How will progress be measured?   How often will we measure and report on progress?

- Improved financial performance: Revenue, Profitability
- Process efficiencies
- Quality
- Customer experience
- Safety, Operations
- Compliance
- Continuous improvement
- Relationships

Client-Specific Account Plans – Key Takeaways

- ✓ A Client-Specific Account Plan can be short and simple or expanded to suit your preferences.

- ✓ It is essential to have an Account Plan for each client.

- ✓ Better to go the short and simple route and put it in place than delaying and not having them.

- ✓ The Account Plan and the Client Charter can be combined in one document and shared with the client.

- ✓ Account Plans are shared with stakeholders so everyone understands what is going on.

- ✓ Account Plans change and should be updated on a regular schedule, for example annually.

Chapter 7: Early-Action Review

In the case of a new customer - or an existing customer that buys an additional product or service - there is usually a clear expectation of how it will work and the value to be received. To be sure the company is meeting those expectations it is always worth checking with the customer. We call this the Early Action Review.

If you have checked into a hotel and the phone rings a minute after you get to your room, you have experienced an early action review. The front desk is calling to see if everything is okay so far. Before you get too far into the stay, how is it going? Of course, for the hotel it is best to find out early (before bags are unpacked) if there is a problem. And to let the guest know they are important.

Waiting too long misses the opportunity to set things straight. Consider the case of a Software as a Service (SaaS) company which supplies business to business software to enterprise size clients. The software requires configuration and implementation before it can be deployed by the client. Typically, the implementation process takes eight weeks. For this company, the Early Action Review is conducted two weeks from the initial kickoff. About one-quarter of the way into the project. This time was chosen as right because it gives the client some time to understand the work being done along with the style and approach of the team. But it is not too late to voice concerns and clarify any misunderstandings.

Following is a sample Early Action Review preparation document.

To:	Client Name
Fm:	Client Success Manager
Re:	Early Action Review

1. Introduction and Purpose

After about two weeks from the start of a project, we conduct an Early Action Review with all clients. The purpose of this Check-In is to:

- See how we are meeting your expectations
- Identify areas in need of improvement
- Gain insights and suggestions

We do this early in the process so we can address your issues promptly – and fix them as needed. The goal is to be pro-active and make sure client expectations are always met.

2. Review Questions to be Answered

Please complete the following questions and return this to us. We will then schedule a call to review these areas in a live discussion.

a. Is the project meeting your goals at this point in time?
b. Are there any surprises you see in how the project is proceeding? *(Please specify)*
c. Is the project methodology clear?
d. Are you comfortable and confident in the Project Team assigned to work with you? *(Please identify any concerns.)*
e. Please identify areas in need of improvement.
f. Is the timing of the project in-line with your expectations?
g. What is your greatest concern at this point?
h. What other issues should we be aware of to make sure we all realize success?

Chapter 8: After-Action Review (AAR)

With many client-vendor relationships, there is an important event that occurs between the parties. In this context that is what we are calling the "action." After the action takes place, it is a natural time for the Account Manager to conduct a thorough review of how it went, together with the client. People from other departments may be involved, too.

An After-Action Review in the software business often takes place when a solution is implemented or activated with the configuration requirements of the client. Once the client goes live with the software, an After-Action Review session is held to discuss the experience and learn the views of the client. Also, to find out if there are any open items that need to be addressed by the company.

It is my preference to have a live discussion with the stakeholders as the After-Action Review session. Sometimes this may not be practical and it can be achieved with an on-line survey where the customer answers a series of prepared questions and gives their feedback in that way.

Let's assume a live discussion is the approach. It is important to make sure everyone is well prepared for the After-Action Review session. An e-mail may be used by the Account Manager to explain the After-Action Review process and provide a brief questionnaire to be completed. The responses to that questionnaire can be reviewed internally before the session to help have a constructive conversation.

Following is a sample communication used for this purpose.

Sample After Action Review

To: Barbara Farmer, VP of Operations

Fm: Great Company

Re: After Action Review Questionnaire

Customer Feedback Software with Different Communication Methods

Purpose

Following the implementation of the Great Company solution for receiving customer feedback, we like to take time to review the work completed and prepare to transition to the next phase of our relationship. We refer to this as an After-Action Review (AAR).

It serves as an organized way to revisit our Client's strategic objectives and to measure, to the extent possible, the degree to which our software helps further those objectives. It's also a great way to gather client suggestions and thoughts.

The questions included here will help us prepare for the After-Action Review session.

The Steps and Methodology

The After-Action Review follows these steps:

a. We supply a list of items to discuss based on our understanding of your strategic objectives and our team's assessment of the solution and the implementation project.
b. Information and questions are presented to the client team looking back at the cycle. Your responses help guide the discussion during the AAR meeting
c. A meeting is scheduled to review and identify action items to be addressed.

After Action Review Questions

Please respond to the following questions:

1. Is our understanding of your Strategic Objectives correct?
    a. Support a process to easily receive customer feedback with different communication methods.
    b. Increase awareness of the customer feedback system among employees.
    c. Improve customer engagement and loyalty.
    d. Have a centralized on-line system to efficiently manage the customer feedback process.
    e. The solution should be logical, easy to use and accurate.

2. Project Management
    a. Did the project meet the go-live dates originally agreed upon?
    b. Did the Great Company team manage your time and resources efficiently?
    c. Did Great Company capture and understand your requirements and use them to configure the software?
    d. Did Great Company understand your requirements for Reports and Dashboards and did we configure the Reports and Dashboards to meet those requirements?
    e. What are ways we can improve the implementation process?
    f. What are your thoughts on ways both of our teams can improve the way they work together in the future?

3. Usability and User Adoption
    a. What feedback did you receive from Executives or Senior Management regarding the software solution and process?
    b. What feedback did you receive from Business Unit Managers regarding the software?
    c. Did Users of the software understand how the software works and how it fits into your company processes?

    d. Were users able to access the system properly?
    e. What are the top two or three pain points that you experienced?

4. Data Management
    a. Was the data transfer and loading process efficient for you?
    b. Are you confident in taking on more of the software reporting on your own?
    c. What suggestions do you have for improving this process?
    d. What other systems that you use would be helpful for us to connect to or integrate with?
    e. Are there other data elements that would be helpful to have included in the system?

5. Training and Help
    a. Do you feel that the Administrator training met your needs?
    b. Do you feel that end-users were adequately trained on how to use the software?
    c. What additional training would have been helpful?
    d. How useful was the on-line Help functionality contained in the system?
    e. Is the User Guide helpful for referring to how to navigate through the system?
    f. If a User Guide was not yet provided, would it be helpful to have?

6. Client Service and Support
    i. Discuss the responsiveness of the Great Company team in supporting your during the implementation
    ii. For planning, please describe changes that you plan to make in the next 6 to 12 months?

iii. For next year, what new strategic customer service and feedback goals do you have?

7. **Product Enhancement Items**
    a. Please share suggested product or process enhancements that would be beneficial to you:

    i.
    ii.
    iii.

8. **Grading**

    a. Based on your experience with our Professional Services team during the implementation, how likely would you be to recommend us to a friend or colleague who needs a service like ours?

With 0 as Unlikely; and 10 as Very Likely: _____

    b. Based on your experience with our Customer Feedback Software since *Go Live*, how likely would you be to recommend us to a friend or colleague who needs software like this?

With 0 as Unlikely; and 10 as Very Likely: _____

Chapter 9: Quarterly and Annual Reviews

Part of the process for successful Account Management is having a regularly scheduled and organized dialogue with customers. Many companies use a Quarterly Business Review (QBR) as an effective way to satisfy this. The client sees the QBR as a set time to discuss the latest developments with the relationship, share news about product developments and address any concerns that may exist. Consistency and preparedness are key ingredients.

We find that clients appreciate the professionalism associated with having structured and consistent QBRs. Sometimes there is not too much to discuss. Things may not have changed dramatically from the last quarter. That is okay. It can be a short review.

In some situations, a quarterly review is too much. If that is the case, having a semi-annual review is perfectly fine. It can accomplish the same goal and be set at a more appropriate tempo for your company. The interval is less important than carrying the review out - consistently.

Edison Partners, (www.edisonpartners.com) a growth equity investment firm based in Princeton, New Jersey, analyzes the best practices of fast-growing companies. A blog post by Alexandria Symos with Edison Partners reported:

> Customer Success done right is a key booster on the revenue rocket, with fast growers investing 6x more in the Customer Success function than their slower growing counterparts. And it's not only the investment dollars that distinguish fast growers; it's also their customer-centric practices and disciplines that yield exceptional

results on critical metrics like retention, NPS and time to value.[5]

Symos describes the review process, such as the QBR, as a success factor that fast-growing companies deploy to set them apart from competitors

> Customer Success plays an important role in the account review discipline, in which scorecard performance is leveraged with the sole purpose of engaging the customer in candid discussion. You'd be surprised how often these conversations reveal the latest shift in priorities, routinely affirm reasons for buying your product and, occasionally, foreshadow the winds of organizational change. It's usually an opportunity to learn something you didn't know about the company, the buying team or their workflows, and always a time in which the customer shines as the star on their journey with your product.[6]

On the following pages is a sample QBR to illustrate the type of content that can serve as the basis for this type of session.

---

[5] Customer Success: The New Superhero of Fast Growing Companies, Alexandria Symos, Edison Partners Blog, August 10, 2019

[6] Ibid

Sample Quarterly Business Review

QUARTERLY BUSINESS REVIEW
Q3 2019: July – September 2019

My Company + Client Company

October 2019

Looking back at the last quarter...

Main Results
- Training of Team
- Final End-to-End Testing of the Software
- Documentation Completed

Issues Addressed
- Reporting templates
- User roles defined
- API activation

Key Objectives for Q4 – October through December 2019

1. Sign off on all configuration items
2. Pre-launch focus group formation and usability review
3. Video help and training items
4. Action plan for surveying users to receive feedback
5. Kickoff plan

Key Objectives for Q4 – October through December 2019

Sign off on all configuration items	Pre-launch focus group formation and usability review	Video help and training items
Deliver requirements document summarizing configuration	Identify focus group members	Script for help and training videos
Sign-off	Recruit 2 alternates	Budget
	One page memo re: goals of the group	Schedule
	Schedule the usability review session	Review production and edits
	Feedback	Finalize video and training pieces and post each one

Key Objectives for Q4 – October through December 2019

Action plan for surveying users to receive feedback	Kickoff plan

Create on-line survey

Create request email to be sent in advance – get buy-in

Create reminder

Launch survey

Identify all teams to be notified of kickoff schedule

E-mail kickoff schedule – check for any conflicts

Prepare and post key dates for kickoff

Video of Jane Johnson announcing the kickoff

Lobby video monitor with countdown

New Items to Consider

- Goals and Priorities
- Any business changes

Looking Ahead

Feedback

In-Progress	
Updates, News…	• New release - April 2020 • User group conference – May 2020

SUMMARY AND DISCUSSION

- Summary of Quarterly Business Review
- Discussion
- Scheduling Next QBR
- Closing items

Annual Review

One of the Quarterly Business Reviews (or Semi-Annual Review) should be an expanded check on the health of the relationship. Let's consider that an Annual Review.

The design of the Annual Review is similar to the QBR described before. It does not have to get into all of the details that have already been discussed in the QBRs. No need to rehash.

What is most important about the Annual Review is to build it up to be seen as a serious meeting and a big deal by your customer. While QBRs might not always receive everyone's attention, the Annual Review is a different matter. The stakeholders should all participate. It is a more formal session.

It is the role of the Account Manager to make sure the Annual Review takes place and everyone is well prepared. It may be appropriate to have the Executive Sponsor participate. This has to be billed as a priority. As mentioned, the agenda for the Annual Review does not have to cover every detail of the relationship. (Although that depends on the style of the Account Manager and the particular client. Sometimes, the details are highly desirable to review.)

The Annual Review should be a time to check-in about the relationship and understand what is most important to the client. It is meant to be that time when the Account Manager shares the key results of the year and gains insight from her client about what they want for the future. A sample Annual Review agenda is shown on the following page.

Sample Annual Review

Meeting Agenda

a. Review of the past year
b. Key results achieved
c. Items planned for and new issues that came up
d. Review of your business strategy and how it relates to our service
e. Business changes to expect
f. Are we supporting this strategy?
g. What are the main goals for next year?
h. Major priorities
i. Timeline for achieving these items
j. Feedback

Chapter 10: Client Satisfaction Survey

Periodic client satisfaction surveys are useful to help understand how you are meeting the expectations of your customers. They also can serve as a yardstick for measuring changes and identify trends.

Asking for feedback is a great way to learn what is working well, where you are excelling and where you may be falling short. The client relationship can be enhanced based on this information by giving you a chance to make changes and focus on the identified areas of importance.

What's more, surveys send the clear message that you care and want to know what is going on. This intelligence can be valuable throughout the organization. It is strongly suggested that Account Managers make client satisfaction surveys part of their routine, structured process.

There may be other client surveys deployed from different departments at your company. That should not prevent you from carrying out the survey focused on client success. Just be mindful of the others, what they contain and when they are sent. And plan yours so they do not overlap in content and timing.

The key is for Account Managers to have a client survey as part of their standard process and to carry them out routinely. The survey can be simple. A best practice used by some successful customer success professionals is to use a survey where customers rate the service or product offering in connection with how it is meeting the client's goals in a set period of time. For example, in the past three or six months. And how confident the client is that your service or product will help meet their goals over the next three or six months. The idea here is to correlate your service with the customer's specific goals and objectives in how they use your solution. After all, that is why they are customers.

There are many free templates available on-line that can be adapted. Also, CRM systems and Cloud-based survey software is readily available that makes this an easy process. We have seen companies agonize over the questions and words contained in the surveys. This tends to cause unnecessary delay and complexity.

Keeping it simple helps to ensure it will get done.

We all know surveys are so pervasive today that they can easily be ignored. The best advice is to keep yours short and concise. It will increase the odds of having them completed in a timely manner and being appreciated by your customers.

Sample Customer Satisfaction Survey

1. How satisfied are you with our service?
2. Do you feel our service is meeting your business goals and priorities?
3. Is our service bringing the value you expect?
4. Would you recommend us to a friend?
5. Please tell us how we can improve.

Qualtrics, a technology company that is a leader in the customer experience management software business, has great information about surveys available at their web site www.qualtrics.com. A description of different customer experience surveys to consider is shown here - extracted from the Qualtrics web site – along with considerations associated with each type.

Types of customer experience surveys

There are a few ways you can measure customer experience through surveys. The first question you need to answer is what metrics you want to use. The most commonly used metrics are:

1. Net Promoter Score (NPS)® – Probably the most popular measure of customer affinity towards your company. Created and trademarked by Bain & Company, NPS is a quick survey that typically asks "How likely are you to recommend [company name] to a friend" with a Likert scale question from 1-10
2. Customer Effort Score (CES) – This metric measures how hard it was for a customer to be able to complete the task that prompted their interaction. This survey question could look like, "How easy was it to deal with our company today?" This survey and measurement system can be useful for post interaction surveys with customer service or support teams
3. Customer Satisfaction (CSAT) – This is a commonly used measure for product and services to rate how happy consumers are with what they purchased. The typical survey question to collect this feedback looks like, "How would you rate your overall satisfaction with the [goods/service] you received?"

then offers a Likert scale question type between 1-5 with 5 being "highly satisfied" and 1 being "highly unsatisfied"

Do's and Don'ts for Customer Satisfaction Survey Design

Properly constructed customer satisfaction surveys and questionnaires provide the insights that are the foundation for benchmarking customer happiness. Depending on what customer metrics you intend to use will determine what type of survey questions you need to ask your customers. Below are a few best practices:

DO

- **Ask for overall company rating first**– This satisfaction survey question gives you great initial insight and allows you to compare to industry and internal benchmarks over time.

- **Allow for open text feedback**– Open text questions allow you to collect open-ended responses from your respondents. You can gain more detail about your customer's experiences and you might uncover new insights you didn't expect.

- **Optimize for mobile**– Many consumers are now completing surveys on mobile devices or within mobile apps, so your survey must be optimized for mobile devices. If it is too complicated for a mobile respondent, survey participation will decrease.

DON'T

- **Ask double-barrel questions**– These questions touch on more than one issue, but only allow for one response. They are confusing for the respondent and you'll get skewed data because you don't know which question the respondent is answering.

- **Make the survey too long**– The majority of CSAT surveys should be less than 10 questions. People won't finish long surveys.

- **Use internal or industry jargon-** Your customers must be able to clearly understand each question without hesitation and using internal or industry jargon is confusing to respondents.[7]

While there are strong opinions about how to best measure the customer experience, for the purpose of this book the most important advice to offer is to be simple and consistent. The Customer Effort Score (CES) is described in detail in the book *The Effortless Experience*. The book suggests that the key to customer loyalty is meeting customer expectations for the services offered with minimal effort. Simply put, customer loyalty is a result of customers consistently getting what they were promised. Full stop.

The authors, based on extensive research show that many companies wrongly focus on delighting customers with extraordinary

---

[7] Customer Satisfaction (CSAT) Surveys: Examples, Definition & Template, Qualtrics, https://www.qualtrics.com/experience-management/customer/satisfaction-surveys/, 2019

service. And that does not produce a positive difference in terms of customer loyalty and satisfaction.

> Companies that can build easy-to-use products, help customers execute a purchase in a simple way, and provide low-effort service on the back end will generate disproportionate customer loyalty returns – especially in a world where the hassle factor tends to be more the rule than the exception.[8]

The Customer Effort Score is attained by asking customers to rate on a scale of 1 to 7, how much they agree or disagree with the statement: "The company made it easy for me to handle my issue."

Research shows that the amount of effort a customer puts forth is highly correlated to their loyalty. Basically, the less effort customers exert to do transactions – such as: find answers, get information, place orders, add or correct data – will produce higher customer loyalty.

The authors conclude that "decreasing effort means higher intent to repurchase, to increase spend, and to advocate for a company." For this reason, companies are finding ways to reduce effort to boost customer loyalty. And this is replacing the notion of trying to delight customers.

Stated another way, to build customer loyalty organizations should focus on finding ways to get rid of the hassles, hurdles, extra effort put forth by customers to use your product or service. Decrease customer effort and you will reduce disloyalty....and increase loyalty.

A key takeaway from *The Effortless Experience*:

---

[8] Matthew Dixon, Nick Toman, and Rick DeLisi, *The Effortless Experience*, (New York: The Penguin Group, 2013) p. 205.

Effort should be reduced throughout the customer life cycle. Our research demonstrates that reducing customer effort in pre- and post-sales customer touchpoints has measurable loyalty impact. The ease with which customers can learn about products or services, make a purchase, and obtain post-sales service and support provides a dramatic opportunity for brand differentiation.[9]

Client Satisfaction Surveys – the kind that best fit your organization – should be included in the Account Manager's game plan. Surveys are a way to receive constructive information in a professional manner.

It is worth noting that surveys can produce unexpected results. There are many examples of situations where clients give more honest feedback in a standardized survey than in other types of communication or meetings.

This can be because some people feel this is the appropriate mechanism for offering candid thoughts. Sometimes, there is a sense that a survey is less personal and the feedback can and should be more honest. Of course, that is a good thing for Account Managers. It is always best to know what customers really think.

---

[9] Ibid, p. 205

Chapter 11: Renewal and Expansion Plan

With a company's strategic accounts – usually the largest and with the most growth potential – it warrants identifying the specific steps to follow to make sure business will be retained and grown.

We will refer to that here as the *Renewal and Expansion Plan*. It is generally an internal plan that is created by the Account Manager in collaboration with other colleagues, such as sales or business development. The content is then presented to the client.

As the title suggests there are two parts to the Renewal and Expansion Plan. First, renew the contract with the client for the same products or services currently being provided. In this, are items that such as:

Renewal Items	Current	Proposed
Existing services/ products provided		
Pricing		
Agreement Term or Period (Expiration date)		
Significant Changes and Enhancements made by our company and available to client		
Coverage (such as the business units or departments which are users of the services and products.)		

In the expansion portion of the plan are items that have been identified over the course of the relationship that may add value for the client. This can include new products or services your company has introduced or supplemental offerings to the core product. In addition, there may be changes that are desired by either or both parties:

Expansion Items	Proposed Terms
Add the reporting and analytics module to the agreement. This would be for administrative users.	
Present the Optimizer Product for the Anchorage team as discussed in the Annual Business Review session.	
Update current product User Guides and create two User Videos	
Introduce Manager Training sessions in conjunction with annual off-site meeting in April	
Develop a Statement of Work for the integration with Friendly Software using the new API.	
Extend the contract for four years from a three-year term.	

Chapter 12: Executive Sponsorship

While the Account Manager has the job of developing and maintaining a strong relationship with the client, it is often a good idea to have an Executive Sponsor (sometimes called Executive Partner) for major accounts. The notion of an Executive Sponsor is a leader from your company has the interest in taking time to speak with and meet with a client because the relationship is of great value. This can help secure and maintain internal commitment to the account management program.

The frequency of the Executive Sponsor's communication with a client can vary based on the number of clients to cover and the number of Executives at your company who will be taking on this responsibility as a collateral duty.

When we talk about Executive Sponsorship programs, we usually consider what the executive will be doing to relate to the customer. That is a major part. But to make it work, we also should think about how the account manager will communicate internally with the executive. That is, to supply current information and keep the executive aware of relevant activities. Having a structured plan for this internal piece is the responsibility of the account manager and is sometimes overlooked.

Noel Capon in his comprehensive book *Key Account Management and Planning* describes it this way:

> The key account manager must manage upward to secure top management commitment both to a customer-oriented key account philosophy throughout the firm and provision of sufficient resources to achieve organizational congruence. An important device used by several key

account directors is the pipeline report. Issued monthly or quarterly, this report details the status of projects with all key accounts and estimates future associated revenue streams. By keeping senior management aware of key account activities, the report has the additional benefit of ensuring that operations personnel are aware of upcoming implementation needs.[10]

Capon adds:

> Executive partner programs generally take the form of members of the top management cadre being assigned to one of the firm's key accounts. In a very real sense, the executive partner 'works for' the key account manager and is part of the key account team engaged in developing and implementing strategy. The last item is an important issue, for key-account/ executive partner meetings should be held when the key account manager deems it appropriate, and not simply because it happens to fit the executive's schedule.
>
> The executive partner can be a valuable resource for the key account manager in developing strong relationships with the key account. Typically, he can engage in conversations at a higher level than the account manager and is able to gain entrée that may be otherwise denied.[11]

It is fine to limit the Executive Sponsor program to a handful of customers to get started. For example, maybe you have identified five members of the executive team to get things rolling. And you

---

[10] Noel Capon, *Key account management and planning: the comprehensive handbook for managing your company's most important strategic asset*, (New York: The Free Press, NY, 2001), pp. 89-90.

[11] Ibid, p. 90.

decide to assign each executive two customers. Then you might summarize the program and responsibilities in a direct way, such as:

- Executive Sponsors will have a call with their assigned client every six months and a personal meeting at least once per year.
- The Executive Sponsor will foster rapport with the client's executives.
- The Account Manager assigned to the client will facilitate the discussion and meeting.
- The Account Manager will brief the Executive Sponsor on developments in the relationship and suggest topics for discussion.

The Executive Sponsorship relationship should be described to the client in a candid, easy to understand manner. What it is. Why and Who. How it contributes to success.

You may benefit by making it clear to the client that this is reserved for special clients. It is flattering to be included in the segment of clients who have an Executive Sponsor.

At the start of the relationship, the Account Manager may communicate with the client and the Executive Sponsor introducing the parties and reviewing what it means.

It is a best practice for the account manager to own the Executive Sponsorship Program. This include matching or assigning executives to clients. Consider it an interview process. Interview the executive to determine the client best suited to work with. In the interview, review the current status of the relationship with the client, key goals and opportunities.

Re: Executive Sponsorship Introduction – Monomoy Corporation

Dear Loretta,

An element of our enhanced Client Success approach is the assignment of an Executive Sponsor for key clients.

This is to introduce Alexandra Stiola, Senior Vice President (copied here), as your Executive Sponsor. Alexandra will be reaching out to you directly for an introductory call in the next week.

The role of the Executive Sponsor is for you to have another point of contact at Monomoy. And to make sure we are helping you achieve your goals.

As you know, we strive to supply great technology and service to help you meet your critical supply chain management needs today - and in the future. Having an Executive Sponsor is a way to make sure we fully understand your priorities and deliver the right results.

Thank you for the trust and confidence you place in us and for the business partnership.

Best regards, Emily Chase

Director of Client Success

Chapter 13: The Scorecard

Measuring progress in Account Management is profoundly important in our structured approach. With a standard scorecard to measure results of the program, we can answer questions like:

- *How are we doing in meeting the goals for Account Management?*
- *How are we supporting the objectives of our organization?*

The solution lies in having a scorecard that is relevant and easy-to-use.

As we have noted throughout this book, simpler is often better. A short, easy to understand scorecard wins out over a complex one. It is fine to consistently measure two or three items that are meaningful rather than be bogged down by ten items that are of moderate value.

Measure and Iterate

By paying attention to the results of our key measurements, we gain insights that enable continuous improvement. As a result, refinements to our services and our account management practices can be made.

It is a good idea to share the scorecard results with the relevant internal managers who are stakeholders at your company.

Taking the time to judge success and identify areas in need of attention is a healthy exercise. Also, having a standardized way to show the value of account management can be powerful in different situations.

A best practice is to have a straightforward scorecard which relates to the priorities of your organization and the account management function. Below is an example.

Sample Account Management Scorecard

The Client Success Manager (CSM) has five specific areas of responsibility. Below is a summary along with the measurements associated with each item:

Client Success Item	Measurement
1. **Client Retention and Contract Renewals.** This is a renewal of the client's service agreement. The CSM is responsible for managing the client renewal process. The CSM reviews with the client the renewal options and terms. In some cases, the renewal will be in the form of a proposal covering the next period. In advance of the contract expiration, a proposal is prepared outlining the terms of the renewal. The CSM prepares the agreement renewal document along with the other relevant forms and makes sure they are processed timely.	Client Retention is measured quarterly
2. **Client Satisfaction and Loyalty.** A goal of the CSM is to have highly satisfied clients. Much of the work by the CSM leads to this result.	Net Promoter Score

3.	**Product Training.** It is the responsibility of the CSM to coordinate product training with new associates working with the client and refresher training for existing associates. Training is done as needed. In all cases, annual refresher training is to be conducted. Refresher training is used to review new functions and review items contained in the latest software releases. It is up to the Client Success Manager to determine if other company resources should be included for the training.	Quarterly Number of training sessions held. Satisfaction scores at end of training. Percentage of Total Clients who have received annual refresher training.
4.	**QBRs and Annual Reviews.** The Account Manager will ensure that QBRs and Annual Reviews are conducted with all of their clients. In addition, the findings and results of these reviews will be shared with the appropriate colleagues at our company.	Number of QBRs and Annual Reviews Completed each quarter.
5.	**After Action Reviews.** Shortly after an implementation project or upgrade is completed, there should be an *After-Action Review* with the Client. The CSM should prepare for and coordinate this session. This should occur within 30 days after the project is finished while the information is still fresh in everyone's minds. The purpose is to review the cycle, what went well, what adjustments need to be made for the next project cycle and allow us to learn.	Number of After-Action Reviews (AARs) Completed each quarter.

Chapter 14: Internal Communication

So far, we have looked at a variety of ways Account Managers work directly with clients to deliver success. Before we conclude, we should note the vital step of internal communication. How we keep our colleagues, managers and leadership team aware of the account management activities.

Of course, this can take different shapes and forms. The level of detail used and tempo is up to you to decide based on your knowledge of the company and the people involved.

The important thing to note is to have a routine way to share information about what you are doing and the findings.

My preference is to be pretty broad with this communication. By not including someone, they may feel excluded. And this can lead to a host of problems. But there can be sensitive information in account management communication. Good judgment and common sense must be applied.

Chapter 15: Summary

We have reviewed twelve items that can add structure to your account management function and make account management a defining feature of your company.

With all of these tools the goal is the same: create value for your organization and your customer.

12 Elements of Account Management Success
1. Welcome Aboard Communication
2. Strategy Statement
3. Account Management Guide - Overall Account Management Plan
4. Client Charter
5. Client-Specific Account Plan
6. Early Action Review
7. After-Action Review (AAR)
8. Quarterly Business Reviews (QBR) and Annual Reviews
9. Client Satisfaction Survey
10. Renewal and Expansion Plan
11. Executive Sponsorship
12. The Scorecard

Appendix 1 – Sample Job Descriptions

Client Success Manager

eHealthcare Solutions - Ewing, NJ

eHealthcare Solutions is always looking for prospective Client Success Managers to join our team. We seek highly enthusiastic, energetic, intelligent and outgoing individuals to sell and manage digital advertising and sponsorship opportunities to both agencies and marketers. The position is located in Ewing, NJ.

This individual's primary role includes:

- Build and maintain strong client relationships
- Assess client needs through active listening and questioning
- Renew and grow existing business
- Generate proposals and presentations in response to solicited and submitted RFPs from existing clients
- Manage insertion Orders and campaign delivery– both new and revised
- Manage, Monitor and optimize campaign delivery to ensure contracted goals are met and we are delivering the best results for our clients
- Proactively work with internal data analytics and reporting to recommend campaign improvements and optimizations

Desired Skills and Expertise

- We require a minimum 2 years of experience in digital ad sales, campaign management and/or advertising agency digital media buying and planning
- Strong written and oral communication skills
- Understanding of advertising industry, media buying/selling – pharmaceutical experience a plus, but not required
- Expertise in standard Microsoft Office programs
- Experience with CRM systems – Salesforce and Digital Inventory Systems – DFP
- Detail-oriented
- People pleaser personality
- Adaptable and eager to learn

Client Success Manager
Radix Health - Atlanta, GA

Position Summary

- We are hiring a Client Success Manager with a passion for client experience and a desire to serve as a trusted partner for our clients. In this role, the right candidate will be the primary relationship owner for a set of Radix Health clients, with the primary objective to ensure value maximization from deployed solutions. This includes working directly with clients to drive engagement with our solutions while creating consistent upsell, expansion, and renewal opportunities.

Why You Should Join Us

- At Radix, you can make a direct impact on access to care, working with medical groups that provide care for millions of patients annually.
- You will work on challenging problems with lots of room for growth.
- You will join a team of people who love what they do, work hard, are intellectually curious, and treat each other with respect

Key Responsibilities

- Be an advocate for Radix Health clients. Empathize with every aspect of the client experience, understand their needs, and translate the opportunities for process improvement, product enhancements, or new solutions to internal teams.

- Establish and maintain trusted advisor relationships with both client executive and operational leadership enabling clients to achieve their business objectives utilizing Radix tools. Serve as the first point of escalation and resolution for client questions, issues, or concerns.

- Drive adoption of and ongoing engagement with Radix Health solutions through a deep knowledge of client workflows and Radix product expertise that enable you to illustrate the platform's business value. Deliver ongoing support, optimization, and relationship management across client base that produces positive, long-term relationships and Radix Health advocates.

- Leverage industry expertise with existing or new analytics to proactively identify issues or improvement opportunities. Assist in the alignment of our technology with the client's business strategy, practices, and priorities.

- Work cross-functionally across geographically dispersed teams of client success, product engineering, and other functional counterparts throughout the client lifecycle to ensure there is a shared journey that delivers a compelling experience and aligns with the client's objectives.

Skills and Qualifications

- Strong client management, project management, operations management and people management skills.

- Ability to influence without authority and demonstrated comfort with ambiguity. You'll need to be able to operate well amid changing business objectives, new product launches, etc.

- Readiness to work in an early stage company environment requiring intense focus, a sense of urgency, and persistence to break through.
- Demonstrated willingness to dive into projects - whether technical, analytical, or clinical in nature - and work with subject matter experts from various teams within an organization to drive results
- Excellent verbal and written communication skills to aid in managing client expectations and responses while resolving difficult issues.
- Ability to prioritize, schedule and organize work – perform under tight deadlines with on-going changes in priorities.
- A willingness to travel; potential for up to 50%

Education and Certifications

- 3-5 years of experience in a health care setting and experience in a provider organization/ambulatory clinic preferred
- 1+ year of experience in a client facing, account management or consulting role with a focus in health care technology & systems preferred
- Bachelor's Degree required; MBA, MHA or a related degree preferred

Client Success Manager

Greenphire6 - King of Prussia, PA

Responsibilities

- Manage client relationships after the successful implementation of new technology programs.
- Drive strategic development of clients' programs and actively pursue opportunities to improve through expansion, enhancements and operational improvements
- Quarterback implementation process alongside Project Manager
- Utilize tools that help serve our clients better and with more focus on tangible metrics
- Demonstrate flawless execution of business strategies for Relationship Management.
- Direct and participate in the development of new features and functionality that may be requested by clients during the sales, implementations, or post-launch process.
- Work with cross functional partners to develop strategies and materials to increase the quality and efficiency of support to clients and users.
- Work with Relationship Management Director on business initiatives and other projects
- Assist in the hiring and training of relationship managers.
- Perform other duties, assignments, and special projects as time or circumstances demand

Qualifications

- Bachelor's Degree or equivalent combination of education and experience
- 6 + years of relationship management experience
- Experience working in the Clinical Trials industry
- Experience in managing your own portfolio of clients
- Extremely articulate, organized, and detail oriented
- Be a self-starter with a positive attitude
- Expertise in Microsoft Office suite and experience with Microsoft PowerPoint

| **Client Success Manager** |
| Corsica Technologies - Centreville, MD |

Corsica Technologies, a leading provider of MSP and Cybersecurity services, provides technical leadership to businesses helping them reach their goals. Corsica is looking for people that are passionate about serving our clients, that want to demonstrate excellence in technology, and are looking to embrace new and emerging technologies on behalf of our clients. Corsica believes in community and serves their clients with a team that works and lives in the same community as the clients we serve.

The **Client Success Manager** position is to maintain strong relationships with an assigned group of clients so that they continue to trust Corsica to support their business IT needs. The Client Success Manager serves as the internal advocate for the client.

Responsibilities

The responsibilities for this position include:

- Develop and manage Corsica's post-sales relationship with assigned accounts
- Continually develop and nurture assigned accounts, identifying and planning for account evolution and growth across the Corsica services portfolio and for the overall success of the assigned accounts
- Responsible for all aspects of Corsica's client success with our services and offerings
- Build and maintain strong, trusted advisor relationships with key contacts within assigned accounts

- Conduct regular meetings with assigned accounts that focus on the client's desired outcomes and contain a strong educational component
- Establish a regular communication cadence with clients based on their status and needs
- Ensure the communication of all service updates, relevant events, newsletters, and social media announcements pertaining to assigned accounts
- Responsible for NPS and C-Sat scores in assigned accounts
- Participate in warm handoffs with sales, implementation, and support as needed and applicable

Competencies and Qualities

Qualified candidates must meet the following job requirements:

- Able to represent Corsica at all times in a knowledgeable and professional manner
- Possess a mix of technical knowledge, intellectual curiosity, and interpersonal relationship building skills
- Strong desire to help, nurture, listen well, and communicate effectively
- Willing and able to take action without being instructed
- Able to find solutions to problems independently
- Bring new ideas to the table
- Able to handle interruptions, changing priorities, and multiple tasks in a calm and professional manner
- Plan, organize, and schedule in an efficient manner

- Able to discern and focus on key priorities
- Works well within a group environment
- Able to provide feedback to other members of the team
- Articulates technical knowledge, where appropriate, without technical jargon or lingo
- Exceptional oral and written communication skills
- Ability to communicate with both technical leaders and business owners
- Hard working and skilled at creative and critical thinking

Education, Experience, and Certifications

- Bachelor's degree in a business-related field and 5 years of work experience, or
- Bachelor's degree in any field and 10 years of work experience

Preferred

- Master's degree in business-related field
- ITIL Foundations v3 certification or higher
- Experience with a Managed IT firm or IT industry knowledge or education

Relationship Manager
CIC Plus

We are looking for a 'go-getter' who is passionate about building lasting relationships, bringing the voice of the client into the day-to-day operations of the business – someone who will embrace the CIC Plus culture, demonstrate the value of our leading-edge technology, and obtain the highest levels of client satisfaction.

As a Relationship Manager, you will be assigned a book of business within a territory and be held responsible for obtaining high satisfaction scores, expanding relationships within your client portfolio, identifying promoters, and retaining revenue. You will also work closely with the Sales Executives on any new opportunities identified within your book.

What we're all about?

Our mission is to improve the lives and careers of HR, payroll, and benefits departments through the use of our world-class, online forms management solutions with employee self-service and best-in-class data management, while providing the best client service in the industry.

Our clients include some of the world's biggest and most innovative brands. At CIC Plus we are a collaborative team who believe in having fun and being passionate about what we do. We treat our colleagues and clients with integrity. We focus on our client needs in order to make sure we can deliver innovative products that they love, helping them find solutions that meet their business challenges. We want to work with colleagues who feel the same way and share these values.

Tell me more about this job

The Relationship Manager is responsible for owning relationships with the client (from C-Suite to Functional level) and will be expected to hold onsite Partnership Reviews to ensure all aspects of the relationship are addressed and any remedial action is taken for issues/challenges. Follow through on actions will be critical. The ability to communicate the CIC Plus key values and talk to product strengths/differentiators during these meetings is a must.

In order to maximize our client partnerships, you will be responsible for creating and maintaining an Account Plan on each of your clients while also obtaining Satisfaction Scores. At the end of the day, the RM should know everything going on within their assigned accounts.

Due to the importance of getting in front of the clients, the applicant must be willing to travel at least 50% of the time for this role.

Purpose of the role

Own and drive the relationship in all functions and levels within client's organizations; including VP and CXO.

Commercial accountability for your designated clients

Hold onsite Partnership Review meetings to ensure health and satisfaction of the account

Re-negotiate terms of contracts during renewal

Prepare and deliver client presentations articulately and confidently

Record, track and monitor each client's satisfaction score with a target of 8+/10 for each of your accounts and create plans to increase any under 8.

Understand clients' diverse, specific business needs

Gain a deep understanding of client experience, identify and fill product gaps and generate new ideas that grow market share, improve client experience and drive growth

Create and maintain client specific benefit cases (including ROI metrics)

Monitor and track system adoption and utilization, by client (i.e. the client's ecosystem).

Work with the Client Success team to understand (and influence) the day-to-day issues that the client encounters and their resolution.

Work with the Marketing team to ensure Client Advocates are utilized effectively through video testimonials, referrals, PR etc.

Work with the Development and Product teams to ensure client feedback and market requirements are understood and considered for roadmap inclusion (Voice of the Client)

Display deep understanding of the CIC Plus value, and collaborate with Sales Exec on new sales opportunities

What traits are we looking for?

Competencies required

Account Management, Relationship/Networking skills, Commercial Acumen, Analytical Thinking, Client Focus, Communication, Self-organizing, Self-motivation, Collaboration, Objective Listening, Problem-Solving, Account Planning, Time Management skills, Contract Negotiation, Conflict Resolution

The ideal candidate will be able to demonstrate:

5+ years' work experience in Relationship/Account Management within the SaaS industry

Proven work experience with HR and/or Payroll background (strongly preferred)

Ability to build strong, influential client relationships (both internal and external)

Ability to communicate passionately, persuasively and effectively in a variety of written and verbal formats, with a wide range of people, including clients and external organizations

Strong collaborator with proven ability to work well cross-functionally

Desire to exceed client expectations

Organization, coordination and time management skills

A Positive, energetic, self-motivated and tenacious work ethic with high work standards

Eligibility to work in the US

Travel 50% of the time

Notes

www.ingramcontent.com/pod-product-compliance
Lightning Source LLC
Chambersburg PA
CBHW021454210526
45463CB00002B/775